Exploring Space

LONDON • CHANHASSEN, MINNESOTA

Copyright © 2003 Two-Can Publishing

Two-Can Publishing
an imprint of Creative Publishing international, Inc.
15 New Bridge Street
London EC4V 6AU
+44 0(20) 7583 5839
www.two-canpublishing.com

Created by
act-two
346 Old Street
London EC1V 9RB

Written by: Deborah Kespert
Edited by: Lucy Poddington
Story by: Inga Hamilton
Consultants: Stuart Atkinson (subject), Sandra Jenkins (educational)
Art director: Belinda Webster
Design: Liz Adcock, Rob and Maggi Howells
Main illustrations: Stephen Holmes
Computer illustrations: Jon Stuart
Line illustrations: Andy Hamilton

ISBN 1-84301-087-9

A CIP catalogue record for this book is available from the British Library.

Photographic credits: p6: SPL/Denis Milon/Allan Morton; p7: PowerstockZefa/Julian Cotton;
p9: NHPA/B.Jones + M. Shimlock; p11: GettyImages/Stone/Joe McBride; p13: NASA; p16: NASA;
p18: NASA; p20: NASA; p22: NASA; p25: NASA.

1 2 3 4 5 6 08 07 06 05 04 03
Printed in Hong Kong

What's inside?

This book is about amazing things in space. Find out about stars, planets and space rocks, as well as how people travel into space and even live there!

What's on the disk?

There are great games to play on the disk. Just zoom around in your rocket ship and visit the amazing things in space. Each one takes you to an exciting game. Try to catch the flying saucer for an extra surprise!

▶ Here's the screen that takes you to your games. Just land your rocket to start playing.

snapshots

Moon

Space shuttle

Planet

Space station

Your picture album
When you play a game, you win a picture for your album. There are four different pictures for you to collect. Try clicking on each one to see it move!

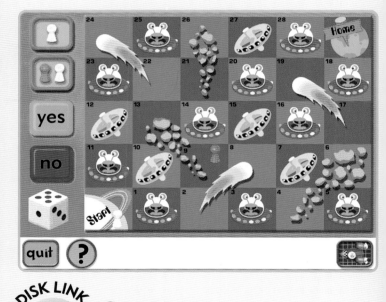

DISK LINK

Space race
Go to the yellow planet to play this fast-moving board game. As you race across space to reach home, there are quiz questions to answer and obstacles to dodge!

4

Space spotter
Go to the space station to play a spotting game on the Moon. Watch what happens when you get your answers right!

Blast off!
Land on the Moon to play a game where you can launch your own rocket. Get your answers right and you're ready for countdown!

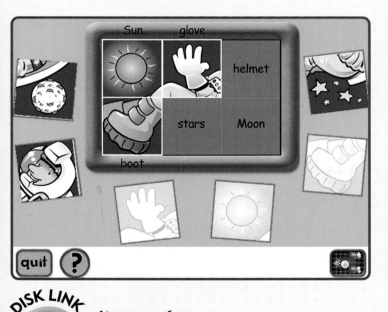

Jigsaw fun
Visit the space shuttle to make two fantastic space jigsaws. To play, match each word to its picture, then drag the pieces into place. There's a printout prize to colour in, too!

It's a bonus!
After finishing two games, meet up with the flying saucer to play a bonus game. Guess each of the things in the telescope and win stickers to make a great space museum scene.

Out in space

When you look up at the clear night sky, you can see far into space. You may spot the Moon and the stars, or even a comet or a shooting star. Space is an enormous place. It stretches much further than you can see!

The Moon is a big, round, rocky ball.

Twinkling stars are millions of kilometres away from us.

Sometimes, you can see a bright stripe across the sky, made up of lots of stars. This is called the Milky Way.

DISK LINK

Catch the flying saucer to see all kinds of space machines close up!

A comet is a giant snowball with a long, dusty tail.

Sometimes, a piece of space dust zooms by, making a trail of light. This is a shooting star.

A pair of binoculars helps you to see into space more clearly.

People point telescopes at the night sky. A powerful telescope makes the stars look much closer than they are.

It's a fact!

Thousands of rocks, called asteroids, whizz through space. Many of these knobbly lumps are bigger than cars!

 # Our Earth

You live on an amazing planet called Earth. It is a ball of rock spinning round in space. Earth is a special place because it has water and air. It's the only planet we know of where animals live and plants grow.

Plants need light and water to grow. Here on Earth, the Sun gives them light and there's plenty of water.

polar bear

walrus

Parts of the Earth are land. People live in towns on the land.

camel

dolphin

Deep oceans cover most of Earth's surface

seal

Rainy places have thick forests with leafy trees.

The poles are freezing cold and covered with ice.

wolf

deer

elephant

giraffe

In hot places called deserts, it hardly ever rains.

lion

whale

penguin

It's a fact!

The Earth travels round the Sun. It races along faster than an aeroplane, but luckily you can't feel it moving!

Tall, rocky mountains reach high into the sky.

The ocean is packed with living things. Fish swim among stony coral, which is the skeletons of tiny sea creatures.

The Sun

The Sun is a huge, blazing ball of fire. It sends out rays of sunshine which give us light and keep us warm. The Sun is a star. It looks much bigger than the other stars in the sky because it is much closer to the Earth than they are.

Fiery loops of gas shoot out from the Sun.

Never look directly at the Sun! It could harm your eyes.

It's a fact!

The Sun is far, far away from us. If you could fly there in an aeroplane, it would take more than 20 years!

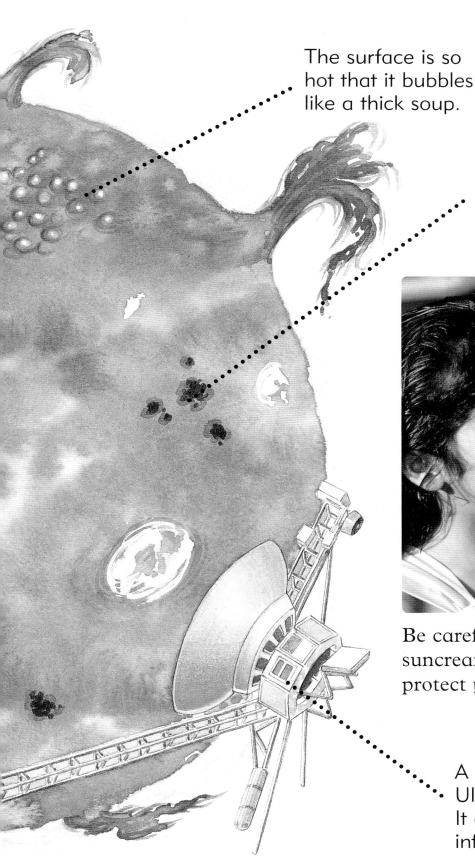

The surface is so hot that it bubbles like a thick soup.

Sometimes, cool black patches appear. These patches are called sunspots.

Be careful in the sunshine! Rubbing suncream into your skin helps to protect you from the strong rays.

A space probe called Ulysses flew to the Sun. It collected all kinds of information.

 # On the Moon

The Moon is a rocky ball which travels round the Earth. It is our closest neighbour in space. The Moon is dry and dusty, so no one can live there and plants cannot grow. A few people have visited the Moon, but they did not stay long!

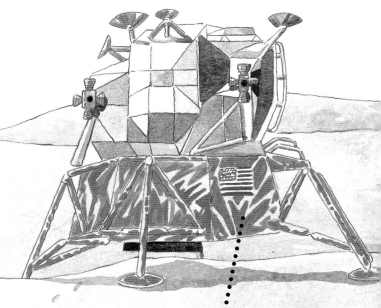

This machine is called a lander. It carried people to the Moon's surface.

It's a fact!

You can shout as loud as you like on the Moon and no one will hear you! This is because there is no air to carry sounds.

When American astronauts landed on the Moon, they planted a large flag in the ground.

DISK LINK

Visit the Moon to play a quiz game and launch a rocket.

12

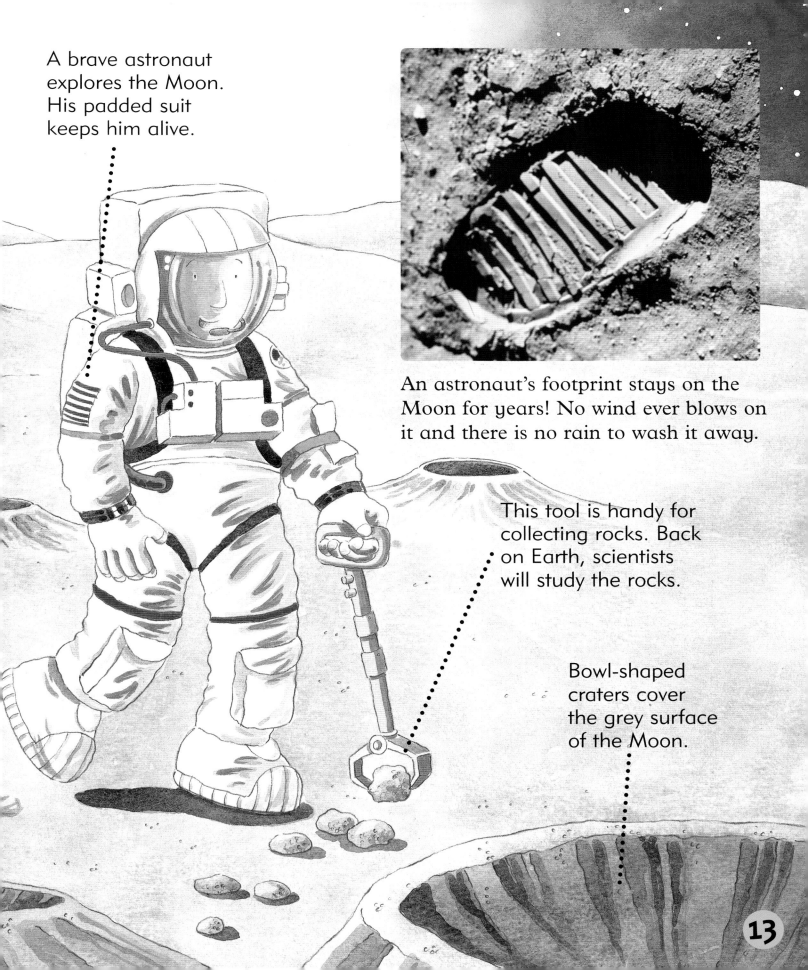

A brave astronaut explores the Moon. His padded suit keeps him alive.

An astronaut's footprint stays on the Moon for years! No wind ever blows on it and there is no rain to wash it away.

This tool is handy for collecting rocks. Back on Earth, scientists will study the rocks.

Bowl-shaped craters cover the grey surface of the Moon.

All kinds of planets!

Earth is only one of many planets in space. These planets are all different colours and sizes. Let's take a look!

Dusty Mars

Rocky Mercury

Watery Earth

Scorching Venus

DISK LINK

Go to the yellow planet to take part in a space race.

Swirly Saturn

Windy Neptune

Dark Uranus

Tiny Pluto

Giant Jupiter

What is the name of the biggest planet.

Words you know

Here are some words for objects in space. Say the words aloud, then try to find the objects in the picture.

planet   **Earth**   **Venus**

Mars   **Pluto**   **Saturn**

How many planets have rings round them?

Astronaut

Astronauts are people who travel into space. They repair space machines and collect information to send back to Earth. When astronauts leave the spacecraft to explore, they wear thick spacesuits which protect their bodies.

Stretchy gloves are useful for gripping tools.

Astronauts sometimes wear special machines to move around in space. It is like sitting in a flying armchair!

A strong cable joins the astronaut to the spacecraft, so he can find his way back.

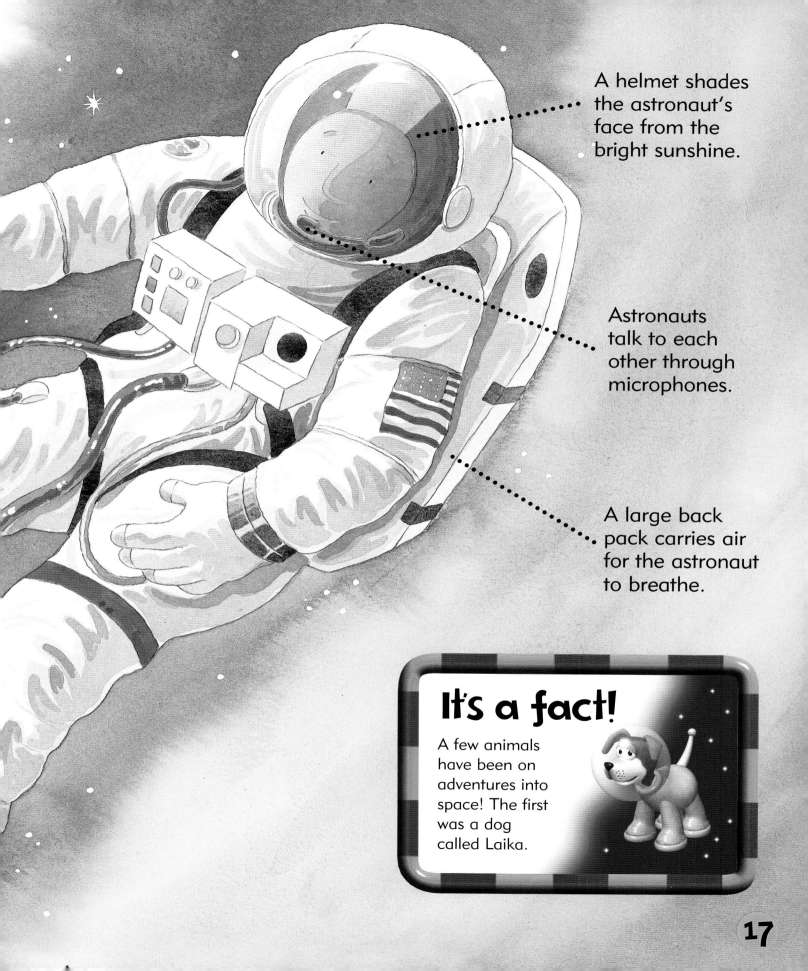

A helmet shades the astronaut's face from the bright sunshine.

Astronauts talk to each other through microphones.

A large back pack carries air for the astronaut to breathe.

It's a fact!

A few animals have been on adventures into space! The first was a dog called Laika.

# Blast off!

A gigantic rocket carries astronauts or satellites far into space. When a rocket blasts off, it zooms into the air at lightning speed. Parts of the rocket fall away one by one. Only the top part of the rocket continues into space.

On the ground, scientists keep a close eye on everything that happens. They talk to the astronauts in the rocket.

It's a fact!

A rocket travels to the launch pad on a mighty machine called a crawler. You can walk faster than the crawler moves!

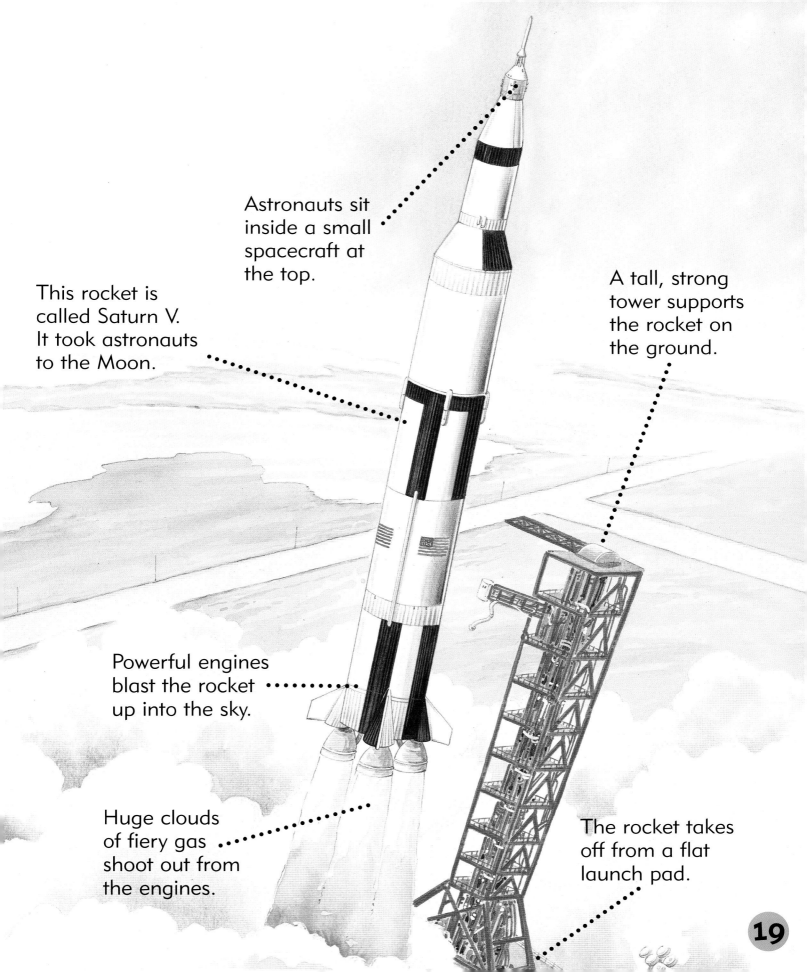

Astronauts sit inside a small spacecraft at the top.

This rocket is called Saturn V. It took astronauts to the Moon.

A tall, strong tower supports the rocket on the ground.

Powerful engines blast the rocket up into the sky.

Huge clouds of fiery gas shoot out from the engines.

The rocket takes off from a flat launch pad.

Moon buggy

A car called a moon buggy is handy for driving around on the Moon. The astronauts take the buggy with them in their spacecraft. When they arrive, they just unfold the wheels, hop in and set off!

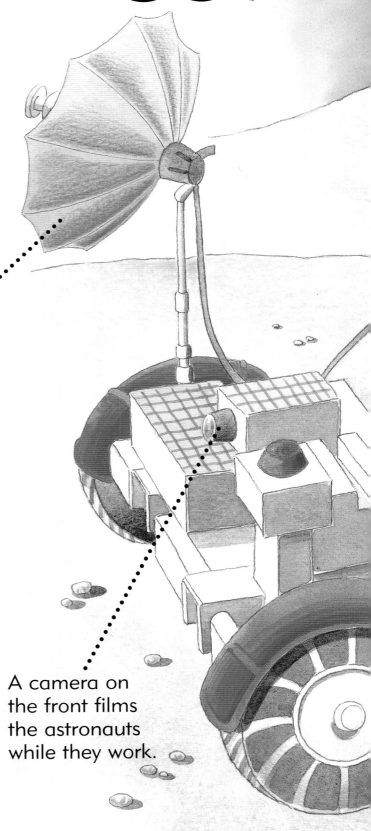

A giant radio aerial sends signals to Earth, so astronauts can talk to people at home.

Some space cars have no driver! This tiny robot car visited the dusty planet Mars. It collected rocks to bring back.

A camera on the front films the astronauts while they work.

A handle steers the moon buggy right and left.

It's a fact!

A moon buggy is perfect for crossing rocky ground, but it moves slowly. You could travel faster on a bicycle!

Bags at the back are for carrying rocks.

Chunky tyres help the buggy to drive smoothly over bumpy ground.

 # Space shuttle

Sometimes, people go into space in a space shuttle. It is like a giant aeroplane that flies into space and back many times. In the big picture, you can see a shuttle landing back on Earth. It has travelled much further than any ordinary aeroplane!

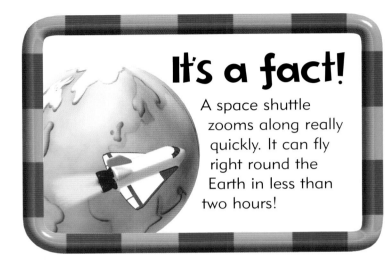

It's a fact!

A space shuttle zooms along really quickly. It can fly right round the Earth in less than two hours!

Two long rockets and a big brown fuel tank help a space shuttle to blast off. These parts soon fall off into the sea.

Astronauts fly a shuttle from the flight deck.

The pointed front is called the nose.

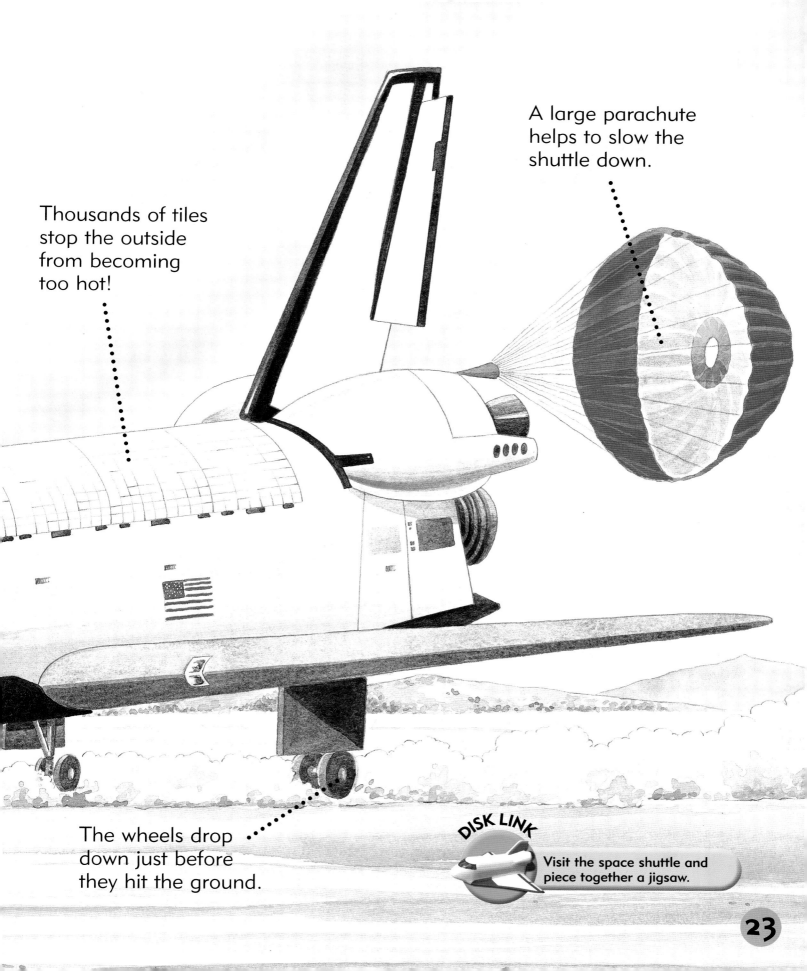

A large parachute helps to slow the shuttle down.

Thousands of tiles stop the outside from becoming too hot!

The wheels drop down just before they hit the ground.

DISK LINK

Visit the space shuttle and piece together a jigsaw.

 Living in Space

In space, astronauts live in homes called space stations. There's no need to wear a spacesuit because it's warm and there is lots of air to breathe. But living in space is tricky because everything floats away!

Washing

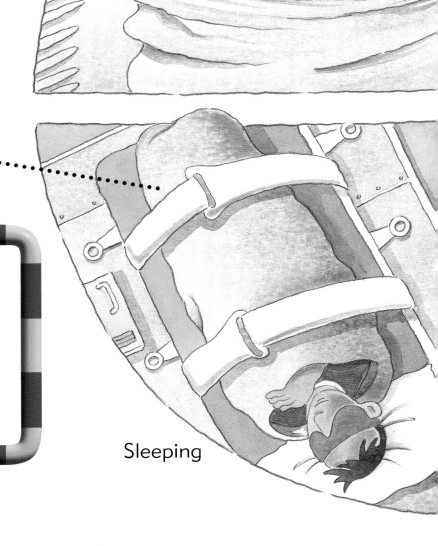

A special bath sucks up the dirty water before it floats off.

Sleeping bags are comfy even upside down. There's no right way up in space!

Sleeping

It's a fact!

Astronauts drink through straws to stop their juice flying away. If the juice escapes, it makes big blobs!

Keeping fit

Astronauts exercise every day. Working out on an exercise machine is a good way to keep fit.

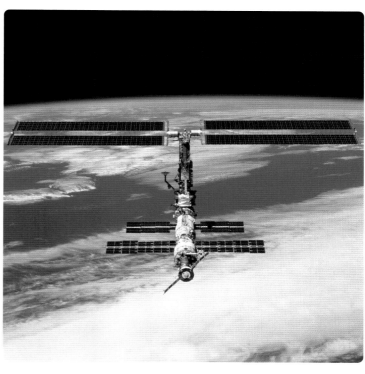

This is the new International Space Station. When it is finished, it will be twice as big as a football pitch!

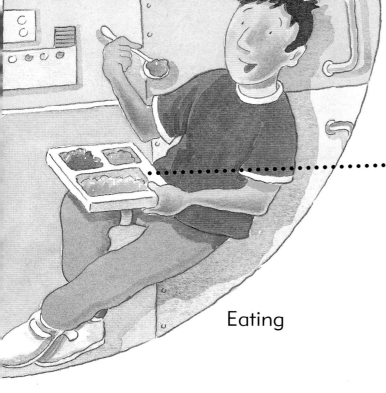

At mealtimes, astronauts eat from trays strapped to their legs.

Eating

DISK LINK

Go to the space station to play a spotting game.

25

Space museum

There are all kinds of exciting things in the space museum. You can look at model astronauts and even a model space station!

What is the astronaut wearing on his head?

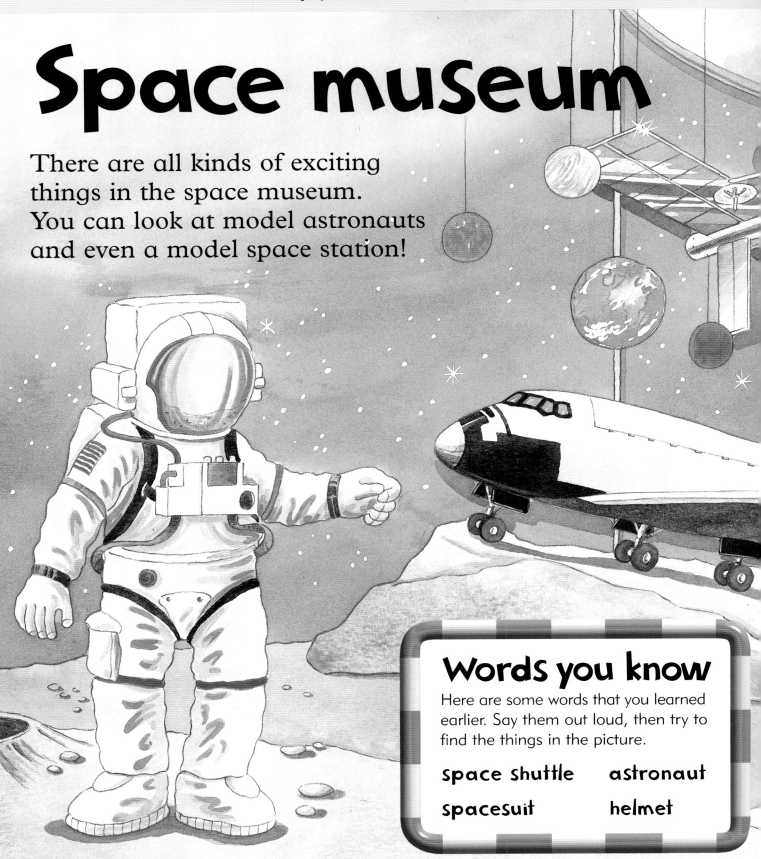

Words you know

Here are some words that you learned earlier. Say them out loud, then try to find the things in the picture.

space shuttle   **astronaut**

spacesuit   **helmet**

Can you see the Earth?

27

What is the astronaut driving?

Footprints in the space dust

Todd was very excited. They'd finally reached the Moon.
Even though his spacesuit was bulky, he felt as light as a feather.
He couldn't wait to get outside and set foot on the Moon's surface.

Todd took a deep breath, opened the hatch and stepped backwards off the lander's ladder. He landed lightly on the Moon's surface, bouncing gently. Touchdown!

"I can't believe I'm here!" he buzzed through his communicator.

"Quite a prize to win, huh?" radioed back Neil, one of his fellow astronauts.

Todd smiled behind his visor. He had beaten millions of kids in a worldwide contest to draw a rocket, and now he was claiming his prize – a trip as a space tourist to the Moon!

"Hey, Todd!" buzzed Neil. "Why don't you take the moon buggy out for a drive?"

Todd didn't need to be asked twice. During training on Earth, he'd loved driving the buggy, but this was for real!

"Just watch me!" shouted Todd, as he set off across the Moon's surface. Behind him the wheels kicked grey dust up into the sky.

Todd drove, leaving the lander far behind. "Wow! Everything is so huge," he thought. "The craters, the rocks, the…" Suddenly he stopped. "The ALIENS?" he gulped.

Squinting into the distance, Todd could pick out two antenna poking up above the edge of a crater. Immediately, his mind was filled with pictures of green-eyed monsters. "Best to sneak up on foot," he decided. With a mixture of excitement and fear prickling his neck, he climbed out of his buggy.

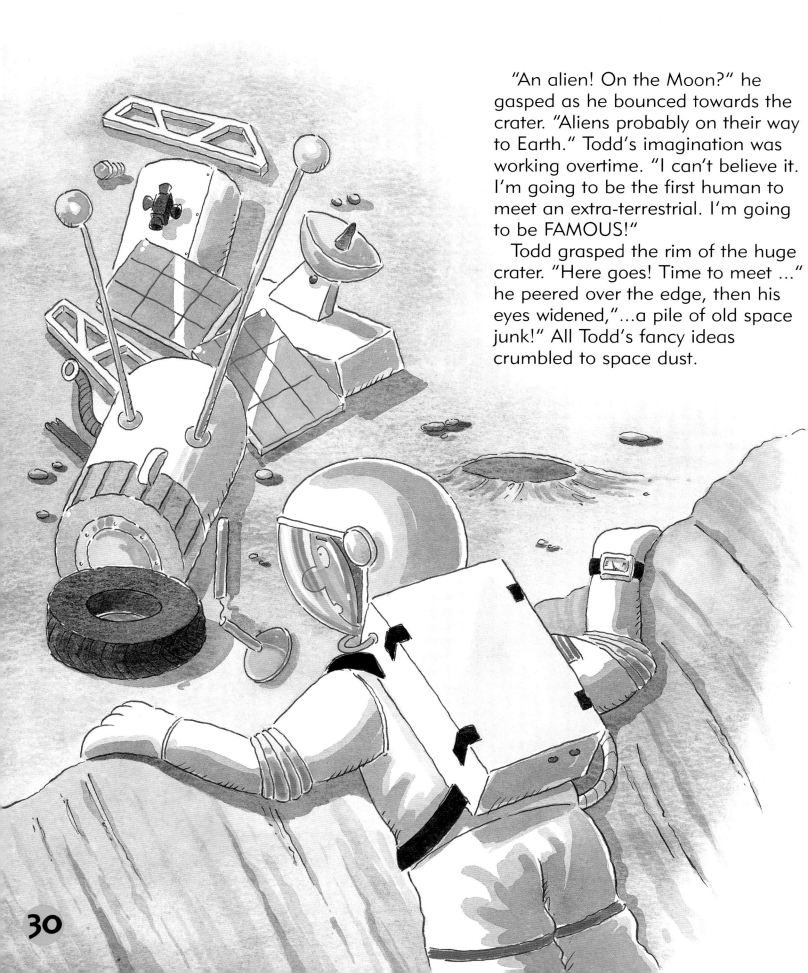

"An alien! On the Moon?" he gasped as he bounced towards the crater. "Aliens probably on their way to Earth." Todd's imagination was working overtime. "I can't believe it. I'm going to be the first human to meet an extra-terrestrial. I'm going to be FAMOUS!"

Todd grasped the rim of the huge crater. "Here goes! Time to meet …" he peered over the edge, then his eyes widened,"…a pile of old space junk!" All Todd's fancy ideas crumbled to space dust.

Disappointed, Todd slid down the massive crater's rocky slope to take a closer look. "It's part of an old lander. It must have been left behind on another mission," said Todd, circling the pile of shiny space junk. He stared up at the tall antenna. "I'm such an idiot," he laughed. "Fancy thinking that they were alien antennae! I've got to tell Neil!"

Todd buzzed Neil on his communicator. "Hey, Neil!" There was no reply. "Come in, Neil!" The communicator was silent. "I must be out of range," he thought.

"Neil will be worried. I'd better get back."

Todd turned to climb back out of the crater and was stunned. "Whoa!" All around him, the towering sides of the crater sloped away as far as he could see. "But which way is back?" Todd wondered.

He looked at his air meter. It was running dangerously low. The hot flush of panic hit him. "I MUST get back to the buggy's emergency air supply."

Panting and sweating inside his suit, Todd tried to think. "Which way back? Which way back?" he cried, turning round and round. He couldn't remember which way he'd come.

"I'm so hot that I can't think! I wish there were a breeze or a shower of rain to cool me down."

Todd stopped. "That's it!" he thought. "There's no wind or rain on the Moon! That means there's nothing to blow or wash away my footprints. Now, all I've got to do is find my own footprints and follow them back to the buggy."

Trying to breathe slowly, Todd looked for footprints. They were everywhere around the space junk, circling round and round.

But he couldn't find the trail that led back to the edge of the crater. Suddenly, there it was. Deep in the dust, on the other side of a pile of space rocks, was a Todd-sized boot print. Dizzy and needing air, Todd followed his footprints back to the buggy.

"At last!" he gasped, grabbing his extra air supply and taking a deep breath.

"That was close," Todd sighed.

"What was close?" Neil's voice asked loud and clear over the communicator. "You OK?"

"Yeah!" replied Todd. He paused. "I'm over the Moon!"

Puzzles and activities

Now try out these puzzles and activities! If you want to do them again, you can print out copies from your disk!

Letter match

Say the word helmet out loud. Which letter does it begin with? Draw a line to match the helmet with its letter. Do the same for the other pictures.

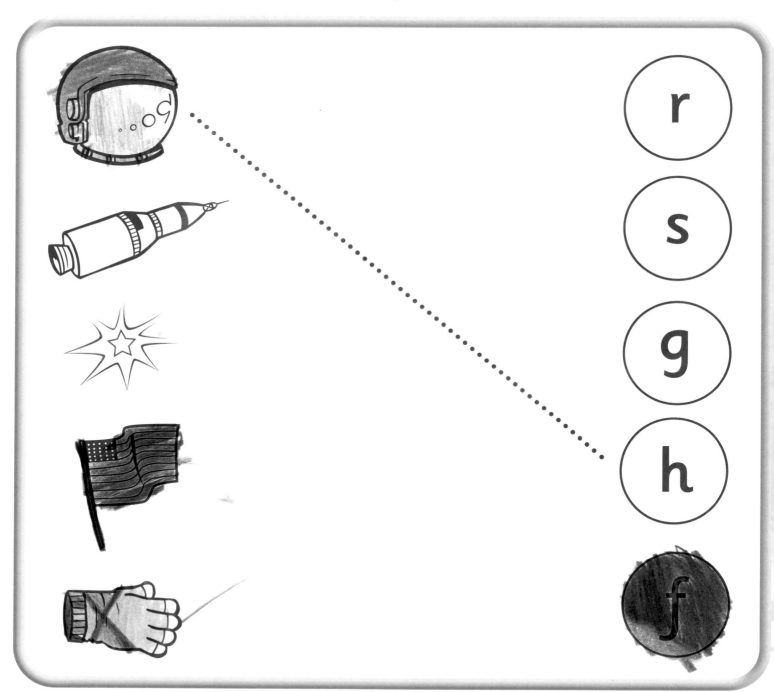

r

s

g

h

f

Out in space!

The astronauts are working on the outside of the space station.
Can you spot ten differences between these two pictures?
When you find a difference, draw a ring around it on picture 2.

Name it!

Can you match all these pictures to the words? Draw a line from the picture of the Earth to its name. Do the same for the other pictures.

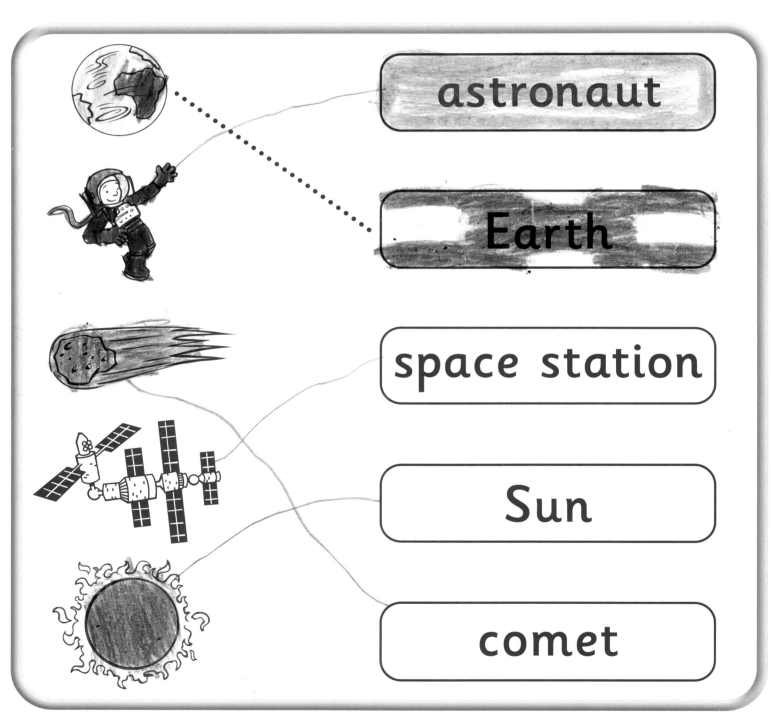

astronaut

Earth

space station

Sun

comet

Odd one out

Look at the row of planets. They are all exactly the same except for one. Circle the odd one out. Then do the same for the other rows.

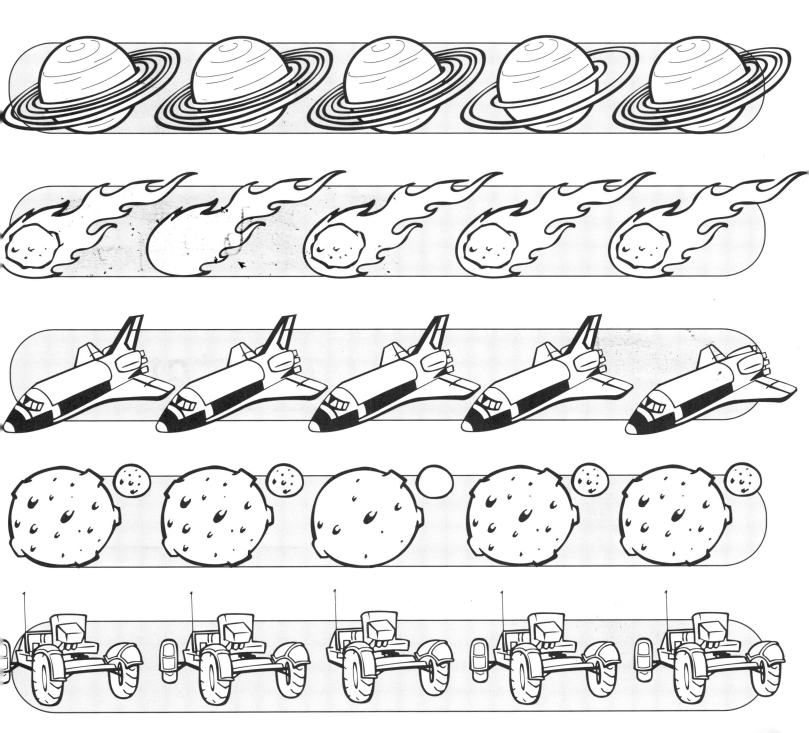

Blast off!

These four pictures tell a story, but they are in the wrong order. Put them in the right order by writing 1, 2, 3 or 4 in the corner of each picture.

Letter pairs

Look at the letters on this page. Draw a line to join the small **r** to the capital **R**. Now match the other small letters with their capital letters.

r   h   t   H

k   o   f

    n

F   T   W

    W   R

K   N

    O

39

Missing words

Look at this picture of an astronaut on the Moon. Now match the words at the bottom of the page to the picture. Write each word in the correct box. The first one is done for you.

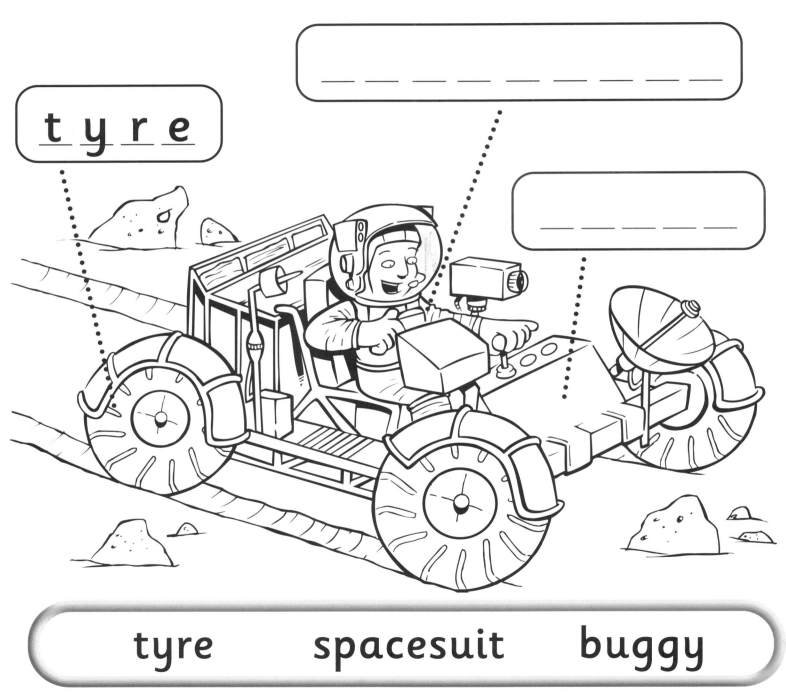

t y r e

tyre   spacesuit   buggy

Now match the words to this picture.

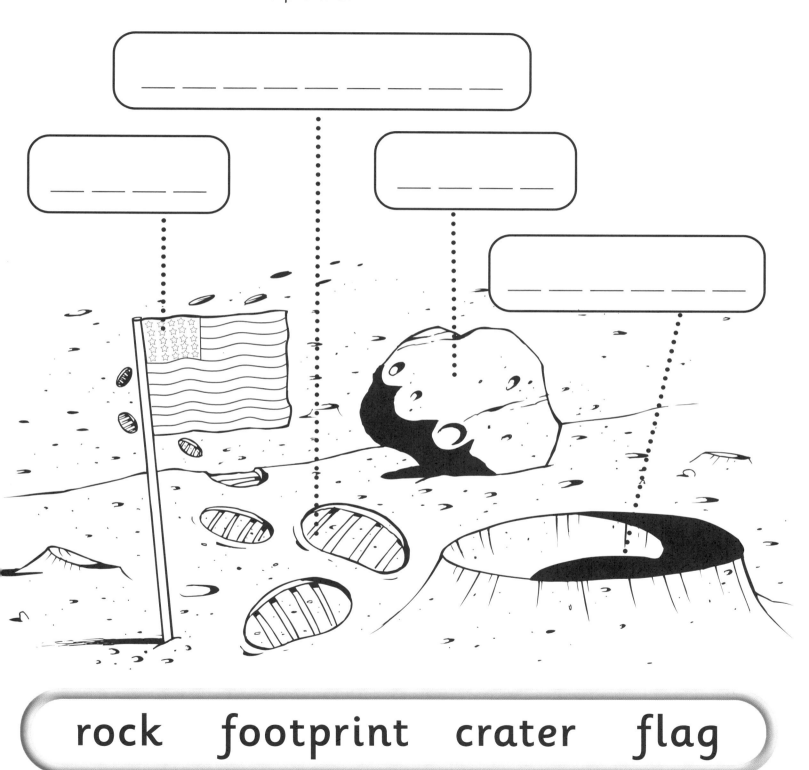

rock   footprint   crater   flag

Up in the sky

You can see all these things up in the sky. Unscramble the letters underneath the first picture to spell a word. Write the word in the box. Then do the same for the other pictures.

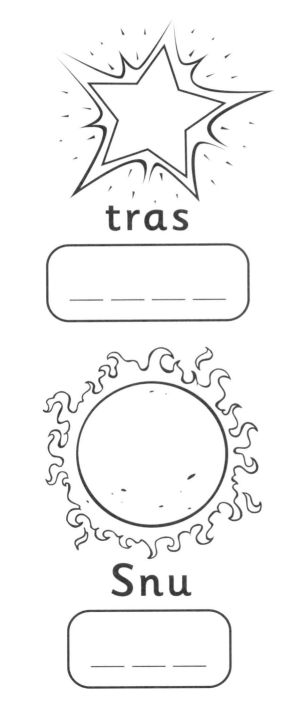

tras

___ ___ ___ ___

Mnoo

___ ___ ___ ___

Snu

___ ___ ___

tomce

___ ___ ___ ___ ___

Space quiz

Read each question, then tick **Yes** or **No** to answer. You can find all the answers in this book! The first one is done for you.

1 Do giant rocks fly through space?

(Go to page 7.) Yes ✓ No ☐

2 Does the space shuttle fly slowly into space?

(Go to page 22.) Yes ☐ No ☐

3 Does a moon buggy travel faster than a bicycle? (Go to page 21.) Yes ☐ No ☐

4 Has a dog travelled into space?

(Go to page 17.) Yes ☐ No ☐

5 Do astronauts drink through straws?

(Go to page 24.) Yes ☐ No ☐

Dotty puzzle

What's in the picture? Find out by joining up the letters
in the order of the alphabet, starting from the letter **a**.
The alphabet is shown below to help you.

a b c d e f g h i j k l m n o p q r s t u v w x y z

Crazy craters!

Draw a line through the maze to help the astronaut drive his
moon buggy back to the spacecraft. But watch out – he must
not drive over any craters on the way or he could fall in!

Space wordsearch

There are six space words hidden in the grid below. Can you find them? Look across from left to right and from top to bottom. Use the picture clues to help you. The first one is done for you.

planet

star

rocket

f	p	a	r	r	a	b
b	l	p	t	o	s	u
o	a	e	h	c	t	g
o	n	l	v	k	a	g
t	e	k	s	e	i	y
a	t	k	s	t	a	r
l	a	n	d	e	r	l

lander

boot

buggy

Answers

page 34

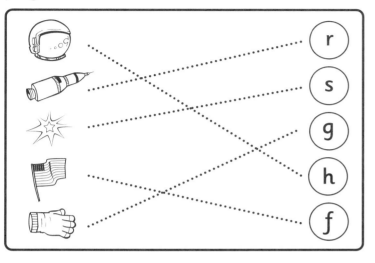

page 35

page 36

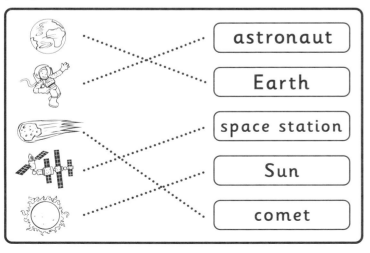

page 37

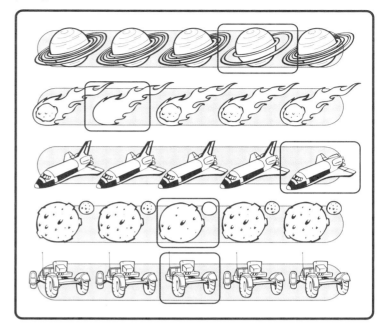

page 38

page 39

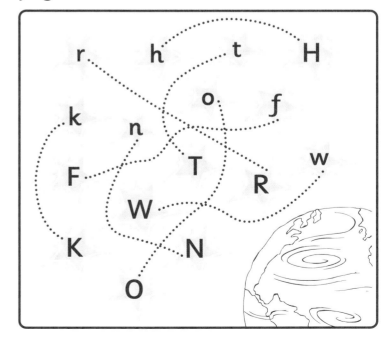

page 40

spacesuit

tyre

buggy

page 41

footprint

flag

rock

crater

page 42

star

Moon

Sun

comet

page 43

1 = yes   2 = no
3 = no   4 = yes
5 = yes

page 44

page 45

page 46

f	p	a	r	r	a	b
b	l	p	t	o	s	u
o	a	e	h	c	t	g
o	n	l	v	k	a	g
t	e	k	s	e	i	y
a	t	k	s	t	a	r
l	a	n	d	e	r	l